EXPLORING COUNTRIES
Spain

by Rachel Grack

BELLWETHER MEDIA • MINNEAPOLIS, MN

Note to Librarians, Teachers, and Parents:

Blastoff! Readers are carefully developed by literacy experts and combine standards-based content with developmentally appropriate text.

Level 1 provides the most support through repetition of high-frequency words, light text, predictable sentence patterns, and strong visual support.

Level 2 offers early readers a bit more challenge through varied simple sentences, increased text load, and less repetition of high-frequency words.

Level 3 advances early-fluent readers toward fluency through increased text and concept load, less reliance on visuals, longer sentences, and more literary language.

Level 4 builds reading stamina by providing more text per page, increased use of punctuation, greater variation in sentence patterns, and increasingly challenging vocabulary.

Level 5 encourages children to move from "learning to read" to "reading to learn" by providing even more text, varied writing styles, and less familiar topics.

Whichever book is right for your reader, Blastoff! Readers are the perfect books to build confidence and encourage a love of reading that will last a lifetime!

This edition first published in 2011 by Bellwether Media, Inc.

No part of this publication may be reproduced in whole or in part without written permission of the publisher. For information regarding permission, write to Bellwether Media, Inc., Attention: Permissions Department, 5357 Penn Avenue South, Minneapolis, MN 55419.

Library of Congress Cataloging-in-Publication Data

Koestler-Grack, Rachel A., 1973-
  Spain / by Rachel Grack.
    p. cm. – (Blastoff! readers: Exploring countries)
  Includes bibliographical references and index.
  Summary: "Developed by literacy experts for students in grades three through seven, this book introduces young readers to the geography and culture of Spain"–Provided by publisher.
  ISBN 978-1-60014-489-9 (hardcover : alk. paper)
  1. Spain–Juvenile literature. 2. Spain–Social life and customs–Juvenile literature. I. Title.
  DP17.K57 2010
  946–dc22   2010009213

Printed in the United States of America, North Mankato, MN.

080110   1162

Contents

Atlantic
Ocean

Canary Islands

Spain is a country in southwestern Europe. It is part of the Iberian **Peninsula** and spans 195,124 square miles (505,370 square kilometers). Spain is the third-largest country in Europe. Its capital is Madrid. It shares land borders with Portugal, France, Andorra, and Gibraltar.

Bay of Biscay

France

Madrid
★
Spain

Andorra

Balearic Islands

Portugal

Mediterranean Sea

Strait of Gibraltar

Gibraltar

Morocco

Spain is mostly surrounded by water. The bordering bodies of water are the Mediterranean Sea, the Bay of Biscay, and the Atlantic Ocean. Spain has 3,084 miles (4,964 kilometers) of coastline. The Canary Islands in the Atlantic Ocean and the Balearic Islands in the Mediterranean Sea are also part of Spain.

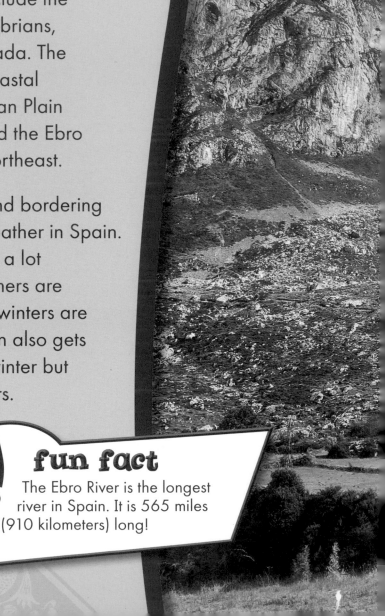

Spain has a variety of land features. There are rolling hills, snow-capped mountains, lush **lowlands**, river valleys, **plateaus**, and islands. Spain's mountain ranges include the Pyrenees, the Cantabrians, and the Sierra Nevada. The lowlands include coastal plains, the Andalusian Plain in the southwest, and the Ebro River Basin in the northeast.

The land features and bordering waters affect the weather in Spain. Northern Spain has a lot of rainfall. The summers are cool there, and the winters are mild. Southern Spain also gets a lot of rain in the winter but has hot, dry summers.

! fun fact

The Ebro River is the longest river in Spain. It is 565 miles (910 kilometers) long!

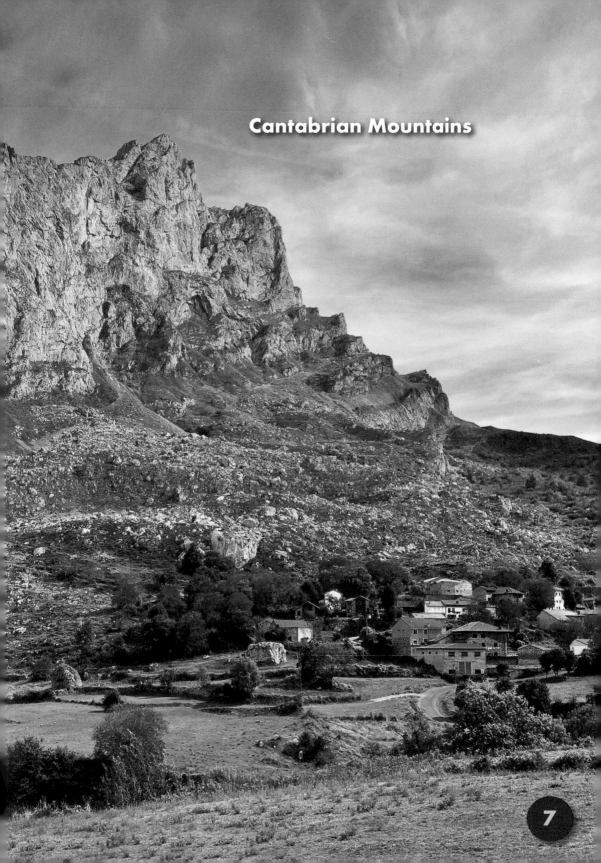

Cantabrian Mountains

Did you know?

The Meseta Central has an average height of nearly 2,165 feet (660 meters).

Much of Spain's landscape lies on the Meseta Central. This large, **barren** plateau extends over 81,000 square miles (210,000 square kilometers). It is dusty, **arid**, and very hot on the plateau in the summer. The wind picks up in the winter, and temperatures can get below freezing.

The Sistema Central Mountains pass through the Meseta Central. The Montes de Toledo and the Sierra de Guadalupe ranges lie in the southern region of the Meseta Central. The Tagus River flows across the Meseta Central and into Portugal.

fun fact

The Meseta Central is the oldest landform on the Iberian Peninsula.

Iberian lynx

Did you know?

The Iberian lynx is one of the most endangered wildcats in the world. Just over 100 adult cats remain in the wild.

Spain is home to many kinds of wildlife. Deer, wild boars, squirrels, and foxes live throughout the countryside. A type of wild sheep called a mouflon grazes in mountain meadows. Wild goats called ibexes climb the mountainsides. Many kinds of fish swim in the inland rivers and lakes of Spain.

mouflon

white-headed
duck

Spanish
imperial eagle

Some of the rarest animals in the world can be found
in Spain. These include the Spanish imperial eagle and the
Iberian lynx. There are only about 500 Spanish imperial
eagles left in the wild. Other kinds of birds in Spain are the
Monk vulture and Eleonora's falcon. White-headed ducks
and marbled teals are common sights in coastal **wetlands**.

fun fact

There are three forms of *flamenco*. They are *cante*—the song, *baile*—the dance, and *guitarra*—the guitar music.

Speak Spanish!

English	Spanish	How to say it
hello	hola	OH-lah
good-bye	adiós	ah-de-OHS
yes	sí	SEE
no	no	NOH
please	por favor	POHR fah-VOR
thank you	gracias	GRAH-see-uhs
friend (male)	amigo	ah-MEE-goh
friend (female)	amiga	ah-MEE-gah

Over 40 million people live in Spain. It is home to many groups of people. Most of the people speak Spanish, which is Spain's official language. Different groups live in different regions of Spain. The **Basque people** live in an area in north-central Spain. They have many languages, the most common of which is Euskera. **Gypsies** settled in the region of Andalusia. They are famous for their enchanting style of music and dance, known as *flamenco*. Jewish **immigrants** are known as the Sephardim. They live throughout Spain and speak their own language called Ladino.

Did you know?
Many buildings in southern Spain have whitewashed exterior walls. The light color reflects the sun and helps keep the houses cool during the hot summer months.

Spanish people have a relaxed daily life. They go to work or school in the morning and usually eat lunch in the midafternoon. After lunch, they enjoy a little nap called a *siesta*. Many shops close during *siesta*. Spanish people usually eat dinner late at night.

Where People Live in Spain

Pie chart:
- countryside 23%
- cities 77%

Most Spanish people live in cities. They use cars, trains, motorcycles, and bicycles to get around. Many people live in apartment buildings. People who live in the countryside often reside in small towns or in houses on their farms.

Did you know?

Few schools in Spain have buses. Most students walk to school or get a ride from their parents.

Spanish children must go to school from ages 6 to 16. Elementary school is divided into three two-year *ciclos*, or cycles. Children study math, reading, and writing. They also take classes in history and science.

At age 12, students start secondary school. They study geography, Spanish, music, and other subjects. Students graduate from high school at age 16. Some graduates go straight to work and some go to university. Spain has some of the oldest universities in Europe. The University of Salamanca was founded in 1218.

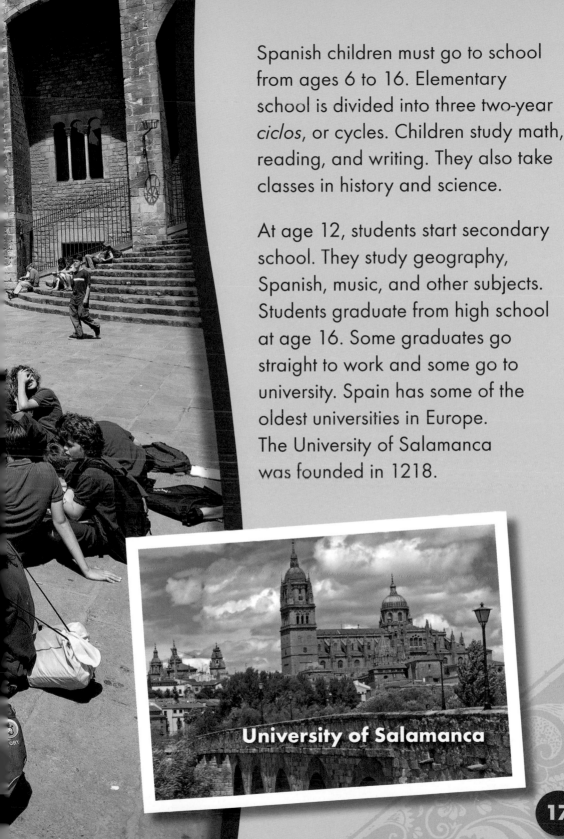

University of Salamanca

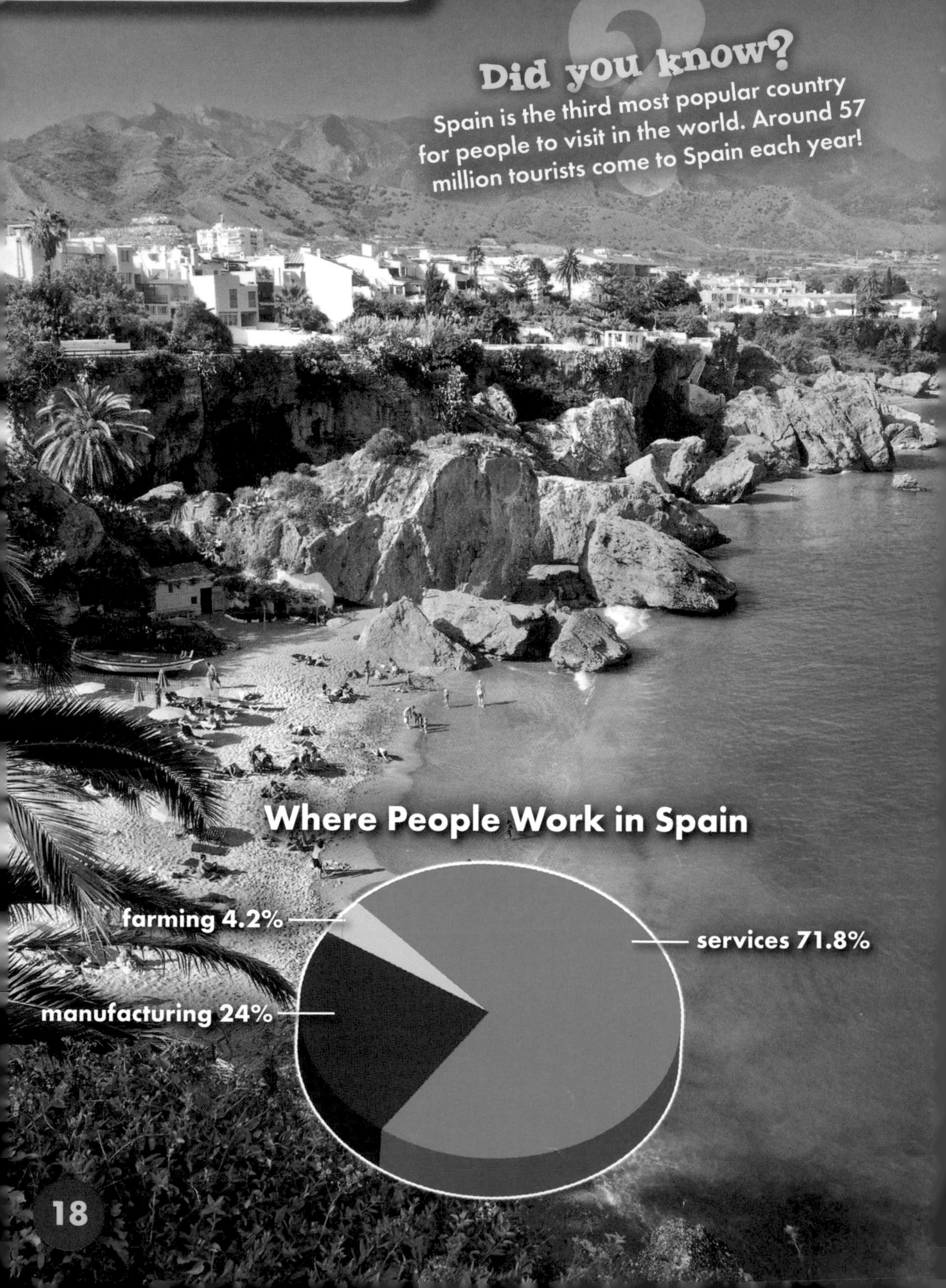

Did you know?

Spain is the third most popular country for people to visit in the world. Around 57 million tourists come to Spain each year!

Where People Work in Spain

farming 4.2%

services 71.8%

manufacturing 24%

fun fact

Spain grows more lemons, oranges, and strawberries than any other country in Europe.

Most Spanish people work in cities. There are many factory and **service jobs**. Factory workers make car parts and machinery, package food, and build ships. Service jobs include jobs in restaurants, banks, hospitals, hotels, and cafés.

Farming and mining jobs are common in Spain's countryside. Spanish farmers grow wheat, barley, and sunflowers. They also grow olives, grapes, sugar beets, and fruits. Miners dig up coal, iron ore, and other **natural resources** to ship to factories in the cities.

People in Spain spend their free time watching TV, hanging out with friends, and going to movies. They also enjoy playing and watching sports. Basketball, tennis, and handball are popular in Spain. The most celebrated sport in Spain is soccer, or *fútbol*. Most students form their own *fútbol* teams and play games against each other.

The Spanish also enjoy motor sports. Many champions of motorcycle and **Formula One** racing have come from Spain. People also enjoy playing checkers, chess, and card games. Spanish parks often have tables set up for these games.

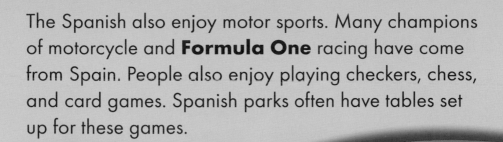

fun fact

Jaime Víctor Alguersuari Escudero of Spain is the youngest driver to race Formula One in the history of the sport. He first raced at age 18.

Jaime Víctor Alguersuari Escudero

Did you know?

Spain produces more olive oil every year than any other country in the world.

paella

People in Spain enjoy eating a wide variety of food. In Spain, lunch is the main meal of the day. One popular lunch dish is *paella*. This one-pan meal is a mixture of rice, vegetables, spices, and meats. The meats in *paella* depend on where the dish is being made. Areas near coasts use seafood. Cities and towns farther inland use beef, chicken, or other meat.

Another favorite Spanish food is chilled soup called *gazpacho*. It is made with chopped tomatoes, peppers, cucumbers, onions, and croutons. Flan is a classic dessert. This custard-style treat comes in many flavors. The Spanish eat light finger foods called *tapas* for dinner. *Tapas* can range from olives in a bowl to small pieces of meat with dipping sauce.

fun fact

Spanish shepherds invented *churros*, which are fried pastries rolled in cinnamon sugar.

churros

gazpacho

Throughout the year, many holidays are celebrated in Spain. In March, people in Valencia celebrate *Las Fallas de Valencia,* or the Festival of Fire. The last night of the festival is called *La Nit del Foc*, or The Night of Fire. On this night, huge puppets are stuffed with fireworks and set on fire.

Nearly all of Spain celebrates *Semana Santa*, or Holy Week. This religious event begins on Palm Sunday and lasts until Easter Sunday. Spanish people observe Holy Week with **processions**. People walk down the street with large floats carrying life-sized figures of saints.

Semana Santa

Did you know?

In Spanish, the word for festival is fiesta, which also means "party" and "feast."

La Nit del Foc

Did you know?

A bullfighter, or *matador*, has helpers in the bullring. Two *picadors* on horseback and three *banderilleros* on foot stay close to the bull. They try to weaken the bull to keep the *matador* safe.

The Running of the Bulls is one of Spain's most famous traditions. It has been happening for more than 600 years. This event takes place during the *Fiesta de San Fermín* in Pamplona. The festival starts with the launching of a small rocket on July 7. The city is alive with music, dancing, fireworks, parades, **bullfights**, and bull running for the next week!

Every morning, brave runners gather at the starting line for the Running of the Bulls. Six bulls are released from their pens, and the runners take off. The bulls chase the runners through the streets to the **bullring**, about 900 yards (823 meters) away. The run only takes about three minutes. Later, the bulls will participate in a bullfight. This cultural tradition is just one of the many ways Spanish people celebrate their country's history.

Fast Facts About Spain

Spain's Flag

The Spanish flag has three horizontal stripes. The top and bottom stripes are red. A yellow stripe lies between them, and it includes the Spanish coat of arms. The coat of arms has symbols that represent many regions of Spain. The current flag was first used in 1981.

Official Name: Kingdom of Spain

Area: 195,124 square miles (505,370 square kilometers); Spain is the 51st largest country in the world.

Capital City:	Madrid
Important Cities:	Barcelona, Valencia, Seville, Zaragoza, Bilbao, Pamplona
Population:	40,548,753 (July 2010)
Official Language:	Spanish
National Holiday:	National Day (October 12)
Religions:	Roman Catholic (94%), Other (6%)
Major Industries:	farming, manufacturing, mining, services, tourism
Natural Resources:	coal, copper, mercury, uranium, lead, iron, zinc, cork
Manufactured Products:	machinery, cars, ships, clothing, shoes, food products, metals, chemicals
Farm Products:	citrus fruits, vegetables, wheat, olive oil, wine
Unit of Money:	euro; the euro is divided into 100 cents.

Glossary

arid—very dry

barren—having few or no trees or other plants

Basque people—a group of people who live in north-central Spain; Basque people speak their own languages and have their own traditions.

bullfights—fights in which a person fights with and kills a bull; bullfights happen in bullrings.

bullring—an arena for bullfights or other sporting events

Formula One—a type of single-seat auto racing featuring high speeds and cars that ride low to the ground

Gypsies—a group of Spanish people who live in Andalusia

immigrants—people who leave one country to live in another country

lowlands—areas of valleys or flat land

natural resources—materials in the earth that are taken out and used to make products or fuel

peninsula—a section of land that extends out from a larger piece of land and is almost completely surrounded by water

plateaus—areas of flat, raised land

processions—crowds of people that move along in an orderly, respectful manner; processions are held to honor important people or events.

service jobs—jobs that perform tasks for people or businesses

wetlands—wet, spongy land; bogs, marshes, and swamps are wetlands.

To Learn More

AT THE LIBRARY

Barker, Catherine. *National Geographic Countries of the World: Spain.* Des Moines, Iowa: National Geographic Children's Books, 2010.

Berendes, Mary. *Welcome to Spain.* Mankato, Minn.: The Child's World, 2008.

Davis, Kevin. *Look What Came From Spain.* New York, N.Y.: Franklin Watts, 2002.

ON THE WEB

Learning more about Spain is as easy as 1, 2, 3.

1. Go to www.factsurfer.com.

2. Enter "Spain" into the search box.

3. Click the "Surf" button and you will see a list of related Web sites.

With factsurfer.com, finding more information is just a click away.

Index

The images in this book are reproduced through the courtesy of: Elena Aliaga, front cover. p. 7 (small); Maisei Raman, front cover (flag), p. 28; Juan Eppardo, pp. 4-5; José Ramiro/Photolibrary, pp. 6-7, 8-9; Pete Oxford/Minden Pictures, pp. 10-11; Juan Martinez, pp. 11 (top & bottom), 15 (top & bottom), 21, 29 (bill & coin); Daniel Prudek, p. 11 (middle); SEUX Paule/Photolibrary, p. 12; Peter Adams/Photolibrary, p. 14; FRUMM Images/Photolibrary, pp. 16-17; Pixtal Images/Photolibrary, p. 17 (small); Slow Images/Getty Images, p. 18; Michael Thornton/Photolibrary, p. 19 (left); Phil Date, p. 19 (right); Jon Giustina/Getty Images, p. 20; Bjorn Svensson/Photolibrary, pp. 22, 26; Ana del Castillo, p. 23 (top); Barbara Pheby, p. 23 (bottom); Christopher Ennie/Photolibrary, p. 24 (small); Magan-Domingo/Photolibrary, pp. 24-25; Felipe Rodriguez/Photolibrary, p. 26 (small); TNT Magazine/Alamy, p. 27.

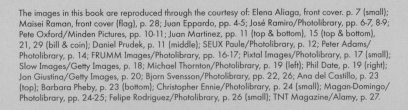